Resistance

Teen Partisans and Resisters
Who Fought Nazi Tyranny

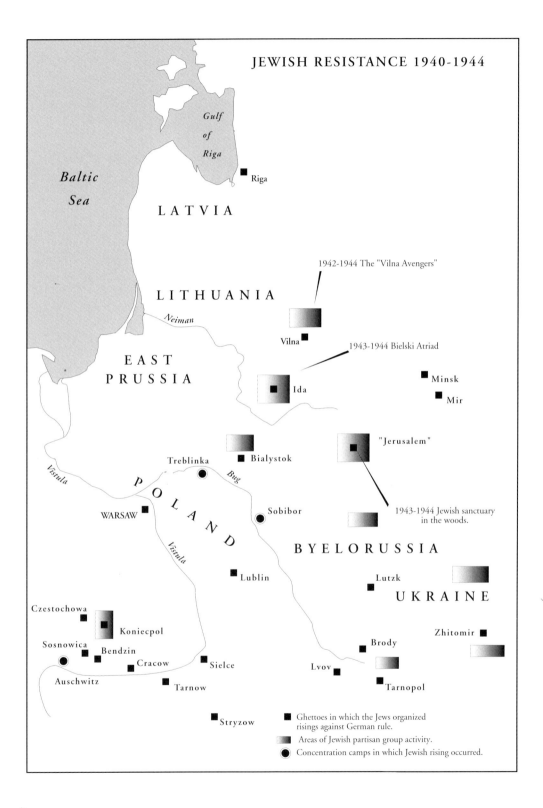

JEWISH RESISTANCE 1940-1944

Baltic
Sea

Gulf
of
Riga

■ Riga

LATVIA

LITHUANIA

Neiman

EAST
PRUSSIA

1942-1944 The "Vilna Avengers"

Vilna ■

1943-1944 Bielski Atriad

■ Ida

■ Minsk

■ Mir

"Jerusalem"

■ Bialystok

Treblinka ●

Bug

P O L A N D

Vistula

Sobibor ●

WARSAW

Vistula

1943-1944 Jewish sanctuary
in the woods.

BYELORUSSIA

■ Lublin

■ Lutzk

UKRAINE

Czestochowa ■

■ Koniecpol

Sosnowica ■

Bendzin

● Cracow

Auschwitz

Sielce

Tarnow

■ Brody

Lvov ■

Tarnopol

Zhitomir ■

Stryzow

■ Ghettoes in which the Jews organized
risings against German rule.

▨ Areas of Jewish partisan group activity.

● Concentration camps in which Jewish rising occurred.

Resistance

Teen Partisans and Resisters
Who Fought Nazi Tyranny

THE ROSEN PUBLISHING GROUP, INC.
NEW YORK

This book is dedicated to my dear family and friends near and far; to the survivors who struggle with what happened to them and their dear ones; among them I wish to thank Dina Abomovics; Moshe Aftergut; Abe and Sari Baron; Efraim (Frank) Blaichman; Yosef Friedenson; Isaac and Rivka Gordon; Leon Kahan; Ed Lessing; Leah Hammerstein Silverstein; Regina Paskus; Hadassah Rublevich; Martin Schiller; and Ann Shore; to the blessed memories of the men, women, and children who were martyred in the Holocaust, may they continue to be a source of strength, illumination, and resolve to those who survive; to those who sincerely strive to learn from the past. With gratitude to God for allowing me to work on this book and to meet so many magnificent people.

Published in 1999 by The Rosen Publishing Group, Inc.
29 East 21st Street, New York, NY 10010

First Edition

Library of Congress Cataloging-in-Publication Data

Resistance: teen partisans and resisters who fought Nazi tyranny / Charles Anflick.
   p. cm.
  ISBN 0-8239-2847-0
  1. Jewish children in the Holocaust—Interviews—Juvenile literature. 2. Holocaust, Jewish (1939-1945)—Personal narratives—Juvenile literature. 3. World War, 1939-1945—Jewish resistance—Juvenile literature.   I. Anflick, Charles.
D804.48.R47 1999
940.53'18'083—dc21   98-33699
                                      CIP
                                      AC

Manufactured in the United States of America

Contents

Introduction

It is important for everyone to learn about the Holocaust, the systematic murder of 6 million Jews during World War II (1939–1945). It is a dark scar across the face of human history. As a student, you are part of the future generation that will lead and guide the family of humankind. Your proper understanding of the Holocaust is essential. You will learn its lessons. You will be able to ensure that a Holocaust will never happen again and that the world will be a safe place for each person—regardless of his or her nationality, religion, or ethnicity.

Nazi Germany added a dangerous new element to the familiar concept of "dislike of the unlike." The Nazis introduced the idea that an *ethnic group* whom someone dislikes or hates can be isolated from the rest of the population and earmarked for total destruction, *without any possibility of survival.*

The Nazis chose the Jewish people for this fatal annihilation. Their definition of a Jew was a uniquely racial one: a person with Jewish blood. To the Nazis, a person with even one Jewish grandparent was a Jew—a person to be killed.

The Germans systematically rounded up Jews in the countries that they occupied during World War II. They built death camps equipped with the most sophisticated technology available in order to kill the Jews. With the assistance of collaborators (non-Germans who willingly helped), they murdered more than 6 million Jews. Among the victims were 1.5 million children and teenagers. These Jewish children, like Jewish adults, had no options. They were murdered because they had Jewish blood, and nothing they could do could change that.

Such a thing had never happened before in recorded history, despite the fact that genocide (deliberate destruction of people of one ethnic, political, or cultural group) had occurred. In the past, victims or oppressed people were usually offered an option to avoid death: they could change their religion, or be expelled to another country. But the Nazi concept of racism did not give the victim any possibility for survival, since a person cannot change his or her blood, skin color, or eye color.

A few non-Jewish people, known as the Righteous Among the Nations, saved Jews from death. They felt that they were their brothers' and sisters'

Three Jewish partisans in the Parczew forest near Lublin, 1943-44.

keepers. But they were in the minority. The majority were collaborators or bystanders. During the Holocaust, I was a young child saved by several Righteous Poles. The majority of my family and the Jews of my town, many of whose families had lived there for 900 years, were murdered by the Nazis with the assistance of local collaborators. Photographs of those who were murdered gaze upon visitors to the Tower of Life exhibit that I designed for the United States Holocaust Memorial Museum in Washington, D.C.

We must learn the lessons of the Holocaust. We must learn to respect one another, regardless of differences in religion, ethnicity, or race, since we all belong to the family of humankind. The United States and Canada are both countries of immigrants, populated by many ethnic groups. In lands of such diversity, dislike of the unlike—the Nazi idea of using racial classification as a reason to destroy other humans—is dangerous to all of us. If we allow intolerance toward one group of people today, any of us could be part of a group selected for destruction tomorrow. Understanding and respecting one another regardless of religion, race, or ethnicity, is essential for coexistence and survival.

In this book individuals who were teenagers during the Holocaust share their experiences of life before and during the war and of the days of liberation. Their messages about their families, friends, love, suffering, survival, liberation, and rebuilding of new lives are deeply inspiring. They are important because these survivors are among the last eyewitnesses, the last links to what happened during the Holocaust. I hope that their stories will encourage you to build a better, safer future "with liberty and justice for all."

Yaffa Eliach, Ph.D.
Professor of History and Literature
Department of Judaic Studies, Brooklyn College

7

chapter one

Resisting the Nazis

The Holocaust is not an easy subject to talk about. The Germans under Adolf Hitler and those who collaborated, or willingly agreed to work with them, murdered 6 million Jewish men, women, and children during World War II. The numbers alone seem too large to comprehend. Tragic and cruel events happened in history and continue to happen today. But no other event was as wide-ranging in scope, as devious in its planning and execution, and as horrifying in its use of modern technology. Human beings and families and communities that had lived in Europe for centuries were destroyed.

The Nazis deceived their victims in cruel ways. Though they treated Jews like animals, Nazis deliberately confused them into thinking that perhaps everything would be fine. They gave false hope to the people they deported, right up to the doors of the gas chambers, which were disguised as shower rooms. Their victims would be far less likely to resist as long as the Germans hid the truth: that they, their parents, and their children were going to be starved, worked to death, gassed, or shot. By hiding this information, the Nazis and their collaborators destroyed millions of people.

Nonetheless, some people did resist. Their resistance took three

(left) A German Jewish family lunches in their garden, Berlin, Germany, 1930. Before the Nazis' rise to power, the day-to-day lives of Germany's Jews were much like those of other Germans.

forms: armed, unarmed, and spiritual. Armed resistance involved the use of weapons; unarmed resistance did not. Spiritual resistance concerned the refusal of a person to be crushed by the Nazis.

Resistance occurred wherever Nazis imposed their rule. In cities, ghettos, and camps people risked their lives to resist. In the forests and cities, resistance fighters known as partisans fought together against the Nazis. Many who resisted were killed. Some of their names are celebrated throughout the world.

Only a minority of Europe's Jews were somehow able to survive the horror known as the Holocaust that lasted from 1939 until 1945. But Hitler's goal of murdering Jews was first imagined many years earlier.

Life Before the Holocaust

In 1918, at the end of World War I, Germany was defeated. The Allies forced the Germans to give up land and pay for war damages. In the 1920s, inflation made German money almost worthless. By 1932, which was an election year, many Germans were unemployed and discouraged.

Hitler and his National Socialist (Nazi) party presented a glorified image of Germany to the downtrodden Germans. He had already published his political ideas in a book called *Mein Kampf*. He wrote this book while in prison for trying to overthrow the government in 1923. In his book, Hitler accused Jews of being both physically and morally inferior, the "genetic" enemy of the German people. He also said that Jews had introduced something into the world called conscience, which weakened people. The most important qualities for a German were to be strong and fierce, he said.

The Nazis convinced many Germans that the Jews, who were less than 1 percent of the population, were the cause of Germany's problems. Not everyone agreed with these antisemitic beliefs, but many hoped that Hitler's Nazi party would help the country recover some of its former glory.

After World War I, daily life in Germany was turbulent. A German bread peddler is thronged by customers, December 14, 1933.

The Nazis Come to Power

On January 30, 1933, Adolf Hitler became chancellor of Germany. Even before winning a plurality in the election that brought them to power, members of the Nazi party would prowl the streets and beat up their opponents, especially Jews.

Two months after Hitler took office, on April 1, 1933, the Nazi Party declared a daylong boycott of Jewish-owned businesses and stores. The same year, Dachau, one of the first concentration camps, was opened to hold political prisoners. The Nazis took control of all German newspapers and radio broadcasts. By mid-July 1933, all political parties other than the Nazi party had been banned.

In 1935, the Nuremberg Laws were passed. These stripped Jews of their German citizenship and forbade them to marry "pure-blooded" Germans. Jews were officially isolated from the rest of Germany society.

Many German Jews thought that the trend against them would eventually be reversed. They considered themselves Germans first and

Nazis form a human barricade on the steps of the University of Vienna in an attempt to prevent Jews from entering one of the buildings, Vienna, Austria, 1938.

Jews second, especially those who had served bravely in the German army in World War I. Over the previous hundred years, the German Jews had steadily won rights that made them equals with non-Jews. Jews actively contributed to all professions, and they often excelled. As each new Nazi restriction was imposed, most Jews believed that conditions had gotten as bad as they could and would not get worse. They waited for the Nazis to fall from power.

Kristallnacht

On November 7, 1938, a Nazi official was shot by a German-born Jewish teenager named Hershel Grynszpan, whose parents had just been expelled from Germany. Two days later, the official, Ernst vom Rath, died. The Nazis used this as an excuse to destroy thousands of German synagogues, rape Jewish women and girls, and kill nearly 100 Jews in a pogrom, a violent demonstration of antisemitism. Organized by the Nazis, it was later called *Kristallnacht,* "the night of broken glass," because the sound of shattering windowpanes in Jewish homes and shops could be heard throughout Germany and Austria .

Many Jews who could get visas managed to leave Germany and Austria after *Kristallnacht.* Many others tried but could not; they were unable to find a country that would accept them. After *Kristallnacht,* conditions in Germany and Austria grew progressively worse for Jews.

War

In 1938, with a plan to create what Hitler called *Lebensraum* (living space for Germans), Germany annexed Austria. In March 1939 Germany occupied part of Czechoslovakia.

Germany invaded western Poland on September 1, 1939, and World War II began. The Polish army was defeated in a matter of weeks. The Germans attacked France on May 10, 1940. Belgium, Holland, Norway, and Denmark were conquered soon after. With each new territory in their grasp, the Nazis imposed their antisemitic policies on the people of those countries.

Adolf Hitler receives a standing ovation from the German parliament, or Reichstag, after successfully annexing Austria.

In September 1939, the Soviet Union invaded eastern Poland, Lithuania, Latvia, Estonia and other territories, where more than 2 million Jews lived. Two years later, in June 1941, the Germans attacked the Soviet Union. The western part of the Soviet Union and all the lands the Soviets had invaded now fell under German rule.

Resisting the Nazis

Despite the power of the Germany army and the pro-Nazi support of many Europeans, some individuals chose to oppose the Nazis. The teenagers whose stories are told in this book endured experiences that may seem unimaginable. Some of them witnessed their fathers, mothers, grandparents, sisters, and brothers being murdered. At times they felt despair. But they refused to give up fighting. Each one, in his or her own way, kept resisting. Each refused to give in to the Nazi idea that their lives were meaningless.

German troops advance on Leningrad in the Western Soviet Union in late summer 1941.

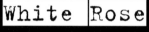

White Rose

At the University of Munich, a group of
students, Hans and Sophie Scholl (above) among
them, formed in 1942. Called the White Rose,
they secretly published and distributed
leaflets denouncing the Nazis and recommending
that Germans sabotage Nazi plans. Theirs was
the only German group that spoke out against
Nazi policies of genocide. The White Rose
expanded to Berlin, Freiburg, Hamburg, and
Vienna. Six members of the White Rose—Hans and
Sophie Scholl; Christoph Probst; Willi Graf;
Alexander Schmorell; and Professor Kurt Huber—
were executed for their activities.

chapter two

Resistance in the Ghettos

In Poland and elsewhere in Eastern Europe, the Nazis forced hundreds of thousands of Jews into ghettos, sections of cities that were usually walled off or otherwise sealed. In the ghetto, thousands of people died of starvation or disease or were victims of shooting. Leah Hammerstein Silverstein was born in Warsaw. She was sixteen years old when she and her family were moved into the Warsaw ghetto.

It was hell on earth. We came to live in the ghetto in October 1940. By March my father was dead, starved to death, literally. These sights—my father and grandmother dying of starvation and terrible hygienic conditions—are a picture that haunts me till this very day. My grandmother was lying on a dirty bed because she was unable already to move without food, and with her lived a young Jewish family with three little children. The mother was soon caught smuggling food into the ghetto, and she was put in jail. And the father was going out

Polish laborers seal off the doors and windows of buildings on the outer edge of the Cracow ghetto, shutting off the Jews' access to the outside world, Cracow, Poland, 1940.

Young Jewish smugglers conduct an illegal business transaction over the ghetto wall. Most smuggling activities were carried out by Jewish youth. Warsaw, Poland, 1940-1942.

with the eldest son (six years old) to find some work to earn some money. He usually came home empty-handed because he was a barber, and very few people needed his services in the ghetto.

I saw these little children turning into little monsters, because when a person is subjected to starvation there are visible changes in their body. First people get swollen, and later on they become distorted. They lay next to my grandmother, who was also in a state of decay. I remember she said to me in Yiddish, "Look in what state I am." And I stood there, a young girl, tears were running down my cheeks. I couldn't help them.

Barbed-wire fences or brick walls blocked off ghetto entrances, which were guarded by local Polish and Jewish police. Some ghettos were tightly sealed; no one was allowed in or out. The Warsaw ghetto was walled in. In ghettos, children and old people usually stayed home, and able-bodied teens and adults went to work. Children often smuggled in food from the "Aryan side," the world outside the ghetto. Others smuggled in weapons.

In 1942, the Nazis began to deport Jews from some ghettos, telling them that they were being resettled.

Resistance

In the ghettos, most of the resistance was unarmed resistance. Weapons were scarce everywhere and were especially difficult for ghetto residents to get. Terrible physical conditions, including the hard labor that Nazis forced Jews to perform in factories or labor camps, killed tens of thousands of people and weakened the survivors. Residents lived on starvation rations in cramped quarters. It was difficult to organize resistance under these conditions. But despite the risks, people in many ghettos formed underground movements or attempted revolts or escapes.

Most of the organized resistance in the ghetto grew out of youth organizations that people in their teens and twenties had joined before the war. One of the groups was ha-Shomer ha-Zair. Its central aim was to encourage emigration to Palestine to start a Jewish homeland there.

Irena Adamowicz

Irena Adamowicz was a Polish Catholic who had befriended Jewish youths in ha-Shomer ha-Zair in Warsaw before the war. A member of the Polish resistance, she served as a courier for the Jewish underground in the Warsaw ghetto, illegally delivering news from outside. In late 1941, Irena and others brought shocking news: The Nazis had slaughtered thousands of the Jews from the ghetto in Vilna (today Vilnius), the capital of Lithuania. The mass shooting took place in Ponar, near Vilna.

This news was the first ever of mass killings of Jews by the Nazis. It dramatically changed the mission of the underground youth movements in the Warsaw ghetto. Leah Silverstein, a member of ha-Shomer ha-Zair, recalls:

When the news about mass killings of Jews reached the Warsaw ghetto, we didn't think about Palestine anymore. We had to think about self-defense. Irena suggested that a delegate, Henryk Grabowski, travel on a bike to the Vilna ghetto and find out what happened. He came back and told us the fate of the Jews of Vilna: at the time of the German invasion of the Soviet Union, thousands of Jews were driven to previously dug out graves, and they were machine-gunned. The resistance groups in the Warsaw ghetto realized that the Germans meant business, the business of killing the whole Jewish nation.

The idea of taking up arms against the Nazis was born the moment we learned about Ponar.

Jewish men are forced to dig their own graves before being executed by German troops, Soviet Union, 1942.

New Resolve

As the news spread about Ponar and other massacres of Jews by Nazis and sympathetic local populations, underground leaders in many ghettos began organizing armed resistance. They wanted to make it hard for Germans to deport ghetto residents because they now understood that deportees were being sent to their death. These activists preferred to die fighting than by mass execution.

In the Vilna ghetto, following the massacre at Ponar, youths organized the United Partisans Organization (FPO) on January 21, 1942. The FPO secretly published a manifesto, or declaration, and passed copies to ghetto residents, urging them to resist being deported and to arm themselves. Most of the people in the Vilna ghetto did not follow the FPO's advice. The head of the Judenrat, the Jewish council selected by the Nazis to run the ghetto, thought that storing arms would only endanger more lives.

In late summer of 1943, Nazis entered the Vilna ghetto and carried out an *Aktion* (a terrifying roundup of Jews for deportation): they liquidated the ghetto. Four thousand women, children, and elderly men were deported to the death camp at Sobibor. Nazis and their Lithuanian collaborators massacred several hundred children and elderly in the same place as the earlier massacre had occurred, Ponar. Four thousand others were deported to work camps. A few hundred FPO members escaped to the forests of Rudniki and Naroch.

But their manifesto had reached other ghettos through couriers.

Couriers

Underground groups in the ghettos sent out many young people as couriers. They carried false papers, illegal documents, and money from ghetto to ghetto, smuggled arms into the ghetto, and helped others escape. Since the Germans had sealed off the ghettos from the rest of the world, couriers were also a primary source of information.

For couriers, danger was everywhere. Local police, German officials, informers, spies, and even some local residents would gladly turn in someone working for the underground and would receive a reward. Many couriers were caught and killed.

In the fall of 1942 Leah Hammerstein Silverstein was eighteen years old. By that time, the Nazis had started deporting people from the Warsaw ghetto in cattle cars. The trains were bound for the death camp at Treblinka, Poland. At that time Leah became a courier for ha-Shomer ha-Zair.

It was decided that I should leave the ghetto and go to the Aryan side [outside the ghetto] and be a courier, or be a link to someone on the Aryan side. And I went with Tosia Altman and a group of young girls who were even younger than I was. My first task was to take care of these young girls and bring them to a safer place. "Safer" was a relative notion, but at that moment, the Cracow ghetto was safer than

Resistance was organized in many ghettos after some ghetto residents learned of the massacres at Ponar and elsewhere. Above, partisans from the Kovno ghetto in the Rudniki forest of Lithuania, 1943-1944.

the Warsaw ghetto. I was given a false birth certificate that was like a ticket to life.

Leah and Tosia brought their charges to Cracow, but conditions there had worsened dramatically.

We couldn't stay in the Cracow ghetto unless we were ready to die there in an attic. So we decided to run, and we ran to the ghetto in Tarnow, which had just had an Aktion. I will never forget the sight we saw there. It was like after a real pogrom: abandoned households, the doors open, broken glass, pillowcases ripped up and, you know, the feathers in the air. Domestic utensils spread all over the place. People in hiding—those who succeeded in not being rounded up.

Life Undercover

After Leah and Tosia got the girls to the Cracow ghetto, Leah continued to work for the resistance on the Aryan side. She managed to get a job at a German hospital in Cracow, cleaning vegetables in the kitchen.

All of a sudden I had to become a Polish girl, with all the Polish mannerisms, which I didn't have. One thing that stood in my favor was that I had a very good command of the Polish language. You see, that was an impediment for many Jews. They didn't speak a pure Polish. There was always a Jewish accent in it, and the Poles could detect you right away. The Germans couldn't, but the Poles could.

The women in that group of kitchen helpers, they were churlish, and their language was foul. Each time I heard them talk, I was red in the face, you know. I was a young girl with no experience, and here I was among women who were prostitutes or who had been maids before the war. Somehow I managed to stay there.

All those years—from the moment I went on the Aryan side—I felt like an actor on a stage, playing a role that I hated. But I had to do it in order to not be detected. You had to learn Polish prayers, which I managed and which I remember to this very day. You had to hide your grief and your sadness. You had to be frivolous. I had good examples in front of me.

And still I was detected by one of the girls. She denounced me to the German. When we came for our weekly pay, she said to the officer, "This is a Jew."

And the German asked me, "Are you Jewish?"

"No," I said, "she *is*." So, you know, he thought that it was a joke, and he didn't make anything out of it.

Another time the kitchen chef grabbed me and put my head on the table. He was preparing sausage for the evening supper. And he put this long knife to my neck and said, "You see, if you were Jewish, I would cut off your head." Big laughter in the room, and I laughed most hilariously, of course. But do you know what it does to the psyche of a young girl? Can you imagine?

Put to the Test

One day on my way from work to the place where I lived, I met one of our members. His name was Tuvia Szajngot. We knew each other from the ghetto in Czestochowa. He was waiting for me. He instilled in me the idea that maybe I could steal a gun. The hospital had Germans, and each of them had a weapon.

Train tracks leading to the Treblinka death camp, 1945.

Vladka Meed

was successfully able to convince non-Jews that she was not Jewish. She served as a courier in Warsaw. She smuggled arms across the Warsaw ghetto wall for resistance fighters, helped smuggle Jews out of the ghetto, and found shelter for them. Above, Vladka poses as a Polish girl on one of her missions to deliver information and money to Jews in hiding. Below, her false identification papers.

And one day it happened. I was scared to death. It was one of the most dramatic experiences in my life.

The room was empty. I grabbed the gun from a holster hanging in a closet and tucked it under my clothes. It was a split-second decision whether I was going to do it or not, and I did it. And here I am with that gun in my hand. Luckily, across from that room was the restroom. I ran in. I didn't know what to do with the gun. So I climbed on the toilet, and there was a window. The window led to a little roof, which was nothing but the top of a garbage bin. I left the gun there, and I went back to the kitchen.

My face was flushed. My mouth was dry. I was trembling. I tried as best as I could to control myself. I succeeded; nobody suspected me.

Later on, there was an alarm. The Gestapo came, and the police came. They arrested the German whose gun I stole. I succeeded in getting the gun out of the hospital. Tuvia came and picked it up. And it did a good job later on in the uprising in the Czestochowa ghetto. When your life is in jeopardy you discover in yourself qualities that you never suspected you had. Until you are put to the test, you never know.

Leah was active in the resistance movement until the end of the war, serving as a courier, contacting partisans, contacting Jews in forced labor camps, and delivering documents to Jews in hiding.

Armed Resistance in the Ghetto

In September 1942, the first wave of deportations from the Warsaw ghetto stopped. Hundreds of thousands of ghetto residents had been deported, starved, or killed. Only about 60,000 remained, and most were not armed. Underground groups, such as the Jewish Fighting Organization (ZOB), guessed the end was near. They collected as many weapons as they could. Arms had to be bought at a high price, most of the time from secret arms dealers or members of the Polish underground. Occasionally they were stolen.

On January 18, 1943, Germans entered the ghetto for the second wave of deportations. They rounded up some 5,000 Jews. But as a large group of Jews were being led down the street, a few of them suddenly threw grenades at the Germans, injuring some and sending others running for cover. Over the next three days, Jewish fighters fired on the Germans. The Germans withdrew from the ghetto and halted the deportations. This success inspired future ghetto resistance; but it also led to a strong German response.

The Warsaw Uprising

On April 19, 1943, at 6:00 a.m., the Germans entered the ghetto under the command of Colonel von Sammern. They intended to empty it. More than 2,000 German soldiers marched in, as did hundreds of German police officers, along with Polish police and pro-Nazi Ukrainians. The German force included a squadron of motorcycles, heavy trucks, soldiers on foot, heavy machine guns, a field kitchen, field telephones, and twelve tanks.

The ZOB had about 600 organized fighters, many of whom were teenagers. Their commander was twenty-four-year-old

Mordecai Anielewicz. Thousands of other Jews had formed groups in bunkers and bought weapons. The ZOB were armed with Molotov cocktails, hand grenades, bombs, rifles, and pistols.

The Germans entered singing battle songs. The Jewish fighters hid behind windows, on balconies, and in attics. When the Germans crossed the place where the three main streets of the ghetto intersected, the Jews suddenly hurled Molotov cocktails, hand grenades, and bombs and fired at them from their hiding places. The unexpected attack sent the Germans running. When they returned to collect their dead and wounded, the Jewish fighters fired at them with pistols. In this first part of the battle, which lasted for two hours, not one Jew was killed. The Germans retreated, pulling out of the ghetto. The fighters were overjoyed.

The next day, a German commander, Major General Jürgen Stroop, entered the ghetto with troops and began to bombard the ghetto fighters with artillery. The ZOB set fire to a German storehouse. Stroop's forces entered the ghetto hospital, shooting and killing the sick. Then they set fire to it.

The ZOB fighters were outnumbered from the beginning. But using their underground network of cellars, bunkers, and tunnels, and going from building to building and rooftop to rooftop, they resisted the Germans for a remarkable twenty-eight days.

On May 16, the Germans took the ghetto and captured the remaining Jews. Seven thousand of them were shot on the spot; the rest were deported to camps. Anielewicz was among those who committed suicide to avoid capture. Some fighters escaped by wading through the sewers for hours until they reached the Aryan side.

chapter three

Resistance in the Camps

The Nazis built thousands of camps, including death camps. Millions of Jewish men, women, and children died in the camps, some of starvation and disease. Most were killed in gas chambers immediately after they arrived at one of several death camps. Auschwitz-Birkenau was the largest. Like Auschwitz, the largest death camps were located in German-occupied Poland.

Resistance in the camps was even more unlikely and dangerous than in the ghettos. Almost no one was prepared for what awaited them in the camps, so no one could organize resistance in advance. In addition, the camps were more isolated than the ghettos, so there was virtually no opportunity to smuggle in weapons or information.

Arriving at the Camp

Upon arrival at a death camp, the cattle cars or passenger trains full of Jews were unloaded. Nazi *Selektion*s took place: those who were considered fit for labor were separated from those who were not.

Of thousands of arrivals, only a handful were selected to work in a camp. The majority—men and women judged to be physically

Bales of the hair of female prisoners found in the warehouses of Auschwitz, Poland, when the camp was liberated by Soviet troops in January 1945.

unable to work, children, the elderly, and women with small children—were sent to their deaths. But first, they were ordered to take off all of their clothing. It would be sorted through and sent to Germany for civilians or soldiers. Women's hair was shaved off, to be made into wigs, mattress stuffing, thread for shoes, carpets, or upholstery for cars and U-boats.

Those selected for death were packed into gas chambers. The gas chambers were designed with a light bulb and a window. This allowed the *Sonderkommando* (prisoners assigned to this grisly task) to make sure that the Zyklon B gas used in most camps killed everyone in the fifteen minutes or so as usual. Then they'd empty out the chambers, pull out any gold teeth with pliers, and proceed to burn the bodies, either in the crematoria—ovens designed specifically for this purpose—or in open ditches. The chimneys would turn the air black, and the stench of burning flesh filled the air. It was the first thing new prisoners noticed.

Those who survived the *Selektion* were now *Häftlungen*, prisoners. They were assigned a number and given striped uniforms and wooden shoes, or clogs, that usually did not fit, and a bowl and a spoon. At Auschwitz, their numbers were tattooed onto them. Many died from overwork or dangerous work conditions. The water at the camps was almost undrinkable, and food rations were intentionally not enough to sustain a person.

Among the inmates of Auschwitz were Sinti and Roma (Gypsies), Soviet prisoners of war, Poles, political prisoners, and religious dissidents, such as the Jehovah's Witnesses. Many died of disease and abuse. All prisoners were mistreated, but only the Jews and Gypsies were singled out for gassing.

There were roll calls, or *Zeilappelle*, in the camp, sometimes several times a day. They started before dawn and often occurred throughout the day. Prisoners were counted each time. Any deviation from the will of the *Kapo* (a prisoner in charge of a work team made up of other prisoners) or *Lagerälteste* (a camp guard) could result in a brutal beating, or, frequently, a "clean punishment": being shot on the spot. Any attempt to resist or escape was punishable by death.

Resisting the Nazis

Even with the barbaric conditions of the camps and the fact that prisoners often spoke different languages, resistance did occur. Political organizations met secretly. One Polish resistance group in Auschwitz smuggled medicine and supplies to help relieve the suffering of their fellow inmates. Those inmates who worked producing German military equipment in factories sometimes engaged in sabotage, at risk of death.

The most dramatic forms of resistance were armed revolts. Those who led these attacks did so out of desperation and a clear sense that all the Jews in the camps were doomed.

Divine Intervention

The camps were meant to degrade and destroy life and to crush the spirit of the inmates. Camp inmates who refused to give up hope or religious faith despite the circumstances engaged in spiritual resistance.

Abie Baron

Abie Baron was born in Warsaw in 1924. He was in his teens when he and his older brother, Shlomo, were deported to the Majdanek death camp in Poland. They passed the *Selektion* and were assigned to work. Abie recalls that whenever he was faced with life-and-death decisions, he somehow figured out what to do. But he takes no credit for making the right choice.

It borders on faith—divine intervention—nothing else. Where would I as a teen get the sophistication to reason without supernatural assistance?

Once, they were taking out prisoners on a transport. Presumably, they didn't need so many prisoners at the camp, so they were going to eliminate them—but they were taking away stronger specimens. It didn't make sense! I saw there was a chance to manipulate the situation. The block master thought that the people on the transports were going to be killed, and he pushed me to the end of the line in order to save my life. But something hit my mind, which I would not have thought of on my own, and I stayed on the line for the next transport.

The block master, Leon, a man from my hometown, yelled at me: "I'm risking my life, you %$@#! Tomorrow, they'll make soap out of you!" I was taken in the second transport. They took us away to a forced labor camp that was not as bad—Jawiszowice, a branch of Auschwitz.

36

Later I found out that, aside from the three transports, the rest of the group were all killed—gassed or machine-gunned—including Leon.

My brother, in his early twenties, was maybe too intelligent. He thought there was no sense in fighting. He lasted in Majdanek only five or six weeks.

Abie was assigned with another young prisoner to the coal mine in Jawiszowice. Using explosives, they broke coal into small pieces and transported it out of the mine by wheelbarrow.

Abie's brother, Shlomo

Coal was the main ingredient fueling Hitler's war effort. We worked close to twelve hours a day without food. At night we were fed soup and given a piece of bread for the next day. I was hungry, thirsty, and tired; I was glad to be finished with my shift.

The German mining engineer, Steiger Holtz—the only name I remember from all Germans—yelled at us: "I'm retaining you for another shift because you didn't work hard enough!" Then he walked away. He was a strong man, about six feet tall.

After a while, we thought it would be safe to leave. We started to go. But Steiger Holtz suddenly stepped out of hiding and began to beat us with a two-inch-wide beam. We ran from him, down the shaft, back toward our work area. He threw the beam at me, and I fell and landed at the shallow edge of a large dirty pool of water on the floor of the mine. Holtz dragged me to the middle of the pool where the water was deeper and stepped on me. The German thought I was dead, but I had some life in me. I was able to lift my head just enough to breathe. I was scared. I didn't know what had happened to the other inmate.

After a few minutes I got up. Steiger Holtz saw me walking toward the shaft. He was amazed, and he blasted me with water from a fire hose going at high pressure. Right away I fell down in pain; but the water washed off all of the muck.

A Polish Christian civilian in the mine helped me. He saw what had happened. He took me aside to the boiler room and gave me something to eat. I had to stay there for eight hours, until the end of the shift. Then

37

*they dragged me back to the camp, to a sick-call room, where there was
somewhat better medical care. I had a fever and stayed there for a week
until it broke.*

*When I went back to work, the other inmate was not there. I
never saw him again. Steiger Holtz saw me and said in German,
"You're still alive?! You are a super-Jew." He had a certain respect for
me. From then on, he used me as a translator instead of
for loading coal.*

*I don't know where I got the chutzpah
to persevere.*

Abie after the war.

Roza Robota was a teenager when she arrived in Auschwitz-Birkenau. In the summer of 1944, she participated in a planned revolt at the camp. Roza arranged for twenty girls who worked in the munitions factory to carry explosive powder out of the factory by scraping it under their fingernails. It was made into small wheels of dynamite, which were carried by the girls in matchboxes concealed in their dresses. They passed them from hand to hand until a Russian prisoner named Borodin had enough to construct a bomb.

The chain of smuggling continued back to Roza. She hid the bombs in the handcarts used to carry to the crematoria the corpses of those who had died overnight in the barracks. Once the bombs were in the crematoria, the *Sonderkommando* stored them for the planned revolt.

Leaders in the Auschwitz underground heard that the Germans had learned of their plan and gave orders to abandon it. The Jewish *Sonderkommando* members, however, believed that their end was near, so they went ahead with the help of some Soviet prisoners of war. On October 7, 1944, using the smuggled bombs, they blew up one of the four crematoria at Birkenau. Six hundred prisoners escaped. All were recaptured or killed. Roza and three other young women were publicly hanged.

More than a million Jews were murdered by the Germans at Auschwitz-Birkenau.

chapter four

The Partisans

Partisans were underground fighters who organized themselves into secret armies that fought against the Nazis. Partisans were often ordinary people who decided to take action. They fought in nearly every country under German occupation. Some partisan groups were more organized than others; some were officially connected to armies or governments in exile or were aided by the Soviet Union.

In the beginning of the war, resistance activity included printing and distributing anti-Nazi literature, forging passports and other documents, and sharing information received through broadcasts heard on illegal radios.

Later, when the tide of the war turned against the Germans, partisan groups began smuggling arms wherever they could find them. Many partisans roamed the forests. They tried to attack the enemy through sabotage, sneak attacks, or direct battle. They traveled in bands of varying sizes. Partisan groups were also active in cities.

There is evidence that members of some partisan groups were anti-Nazi but also antisemitic, though some dispute this. To join a group you usually had to have a weapon, but weapons were difficult to get. Non-Jewish partisans sometimes robbed Jewish partisans of

Members of the French resistance. As in other Nazi-occupied countries, resistance in France was widespread, with many ordinary people joining the fight against the Nazis.

their weapons and killed them. Some Jews became leaders in these groups, but usually they had to hide their Jewish identity.

Living in the Forest

There were many Jewish partisan groups in Eastern Europe, including Polish groups, and thousands of Jewish fighters among the ranks of Russian partisan groups. Jewish partisans were also members of partisan groups in Byelorussia and Lithuania. Their non-Jewish counterparts had trained military officers among their ranks. They had the support of their families and communities. The Jewish partisans had no one to go home to.

Frank Blaichman was sixteen years old at the start of the war. He came from a religious family in the town of Kamionka, Poland.

In my town we heard rumors that the Germans were deporting Jewish communities and ghettos to death camps daily. We felt we were next in line, that it was just a matter of time. I was a young man then, not quite twenty, but I promised myself that I would not go freely, no matter what. I managed to say goodbye to my loved ones, and I ran away.

It was October 1942. I had a promise from a Polish farmer, Alexander Glos, from the village of Kerzowka. I knew him from before. He said that if I needed to hide I could stay with him and his family. My friend Yankel and I first ran away to a castle in Kozlowka which belonged to Baron Zamoinski. There were two Jewish boys working as slave laborers there. We went to warn them of the deportation, but they already knew. They asked the head housekeeper if they could give us food and shelter for the night, and she agreed.

Frank Blaichman

At about 5:00 AM the next morning we went to a young forest near a roadway where we rested and waited for daybreak. We heard whispering voices around us. Upon investigation we found over twenty men who had also run away and come here for the same reason: to find out more information about the deportation and the fate of our loved ones.

We were now between twenty-five and thirty men, and we banded together. We chose two blond-haired, blue-eyed boys to investigate the deportation further. They returned with information they'd heard from a Polish farmer who was passing by on horse and wagon. They learned that the deportation had occurred. The Germans entered the town with the help of the Polish police. They chased all the Jewish families out of their homes. Whoever could not run fast enough was shot and killed on the spot. The rest were sent off to Lubartow. The rumors that we so feared had become a reality. We sat in a circle debating what to do.

42

The majority decided to join their families in Lubartow. My feeling was that if there was a ghetto I could always get in, but if I had to escape it might be too late. I also had Farmer Glos's promise in mind. They tried to convince me, and I felt very confused. I was the youngest among this group of men. At 3:00 PM they began their trip to Lubartow. I actually began walking with them. However, when I saw the church spire of Lubartow several miles away, I was struck by reality. I had promised myself not to go to any ghetto or camp freely. I asked my friend Yankel to join me. He said no. I said, "Good-bye and be healthy" to all of them.

I was now really alone and started crying. I went to the Glos farm. They took me in and treated me like their family. They asked me no questions. They gave me food and told me to sleep. I said, "Let me sleep in the barn," knowing that if I was discovered in their house they would be shot. I couldn't sleep. The next morning, the farmer told me more bad news: All the Jews from Kamionka were put on trains, destination unknown. I visited my town to see for myself what happened. I saw a little boy named Mottle who told me his parents were hiding in the forest with others. I then told Farmer Glos I needed to go away for a few days. He said, "Be careful, and go with God."

I went to the Bratnik forest and there I found a campsite with about 100 Jewish men and women living under the most primitive conditions in bunkers dug out under the ground. Quickly we became bound together. I was fortunate to find my cousin Efraim Levine and his little brother, Usha.

One day some of us went into the nearby village to buy food. When the Polish peasants saw us they began to sound an alarm. They beat their pots and pans, and beat on their tin roofs with sticks all the while screaming "Rzide!"—Jews. They chased after us with pitchforks and axes. We all ran away unharmed, but we were shocked. We did not expect the peasants would treat us as they did. It was at this moment of grim reality that we realized: We must organize in order to survive.

Under the leadership of Yankel Klerrer we began to search for firearms. We traveled many miles every day looking for weapons, but found only dead ends.

One terrible day we returned to our campsite to find it had been

Members of the French resistance parade a beaten-up collaborator before the citizens of Aix-la-Chapelle, France, August 21, 1944.

raided. All of our bunkers had been blown up by the Germans. Eighty percent of our group had been murdered. There are no words to express how we felt. The only thing we could do was to bury the dead and say Kaddish, the prayer for the dead. We then swore on their graves that we would avenge our brothers.

Gaining Strength

A few weeks later, in December 1942, we were standing around a fire baking potatoes when an old friend, Chaim, suddenly showed up, like an angel. He told me he had a job as a carpenter with a Polish group. The farmer there bragged about how many guns he had collected from the Polish army. When the Germans had defeated them, they had thrown their guns all over the countryside.

We organized twelve men to go at night to "negotiate." We had pitchforks, and I had a small pistol. Shabse was a tall dark guy with a mustache, and I was tall, skinny, and with a mustache. I had also gotten a coat from a Polish policeman. We looked official. The farmer, Lemenchek, opened the door in his long underwear. I spoke fluent Polish. I put the flashlight on Shabse, who was impressive-looking.

I told the farmer, "We are Russian paratroopers fighting the Germans, and we came here to organize a partisan fighting unit." We'd heard that he had hidden a cache of firearms. We wanted him to give us the arms willingly because the Germans were also the enemy of the Polish people. At that point he said, "Come with me." He took us to the barn. He pulled out a handgun, then a rifle from the thatched roof, and ammunition. I gave it to my men. Another found a new rifle, covered with grease, buried in the snow. I walked over to

The aftermath of a sabotage by French Resistance fighters of a French freight train in the Soane and Loire region, March 4, 1944.

Members of the Bielski Atriad at the family camp in
Naliboki forest in Byelorussia, 1943-44

*Lemenchek's neighbor, Piotr, and gave him the same speech. That
night we got six guns from five different neighbors.*

*We captured two collaborators. From them we learned a wealth
of information. They had been organized and trained by the
Germans to hunt for Jews and to threaten and spy on Polish
peasants; whoever would help a Jew would be killed with their
family on the spot. They admitted to us that they were the ones who
had led the Germans to our campsite on the first raid. They supplied
us with the names of other collaborators and even their passwords.
With this information, we managed to capture many collaborators,
and we punished them accordingly.*

*This was our first victory, and a turning point in our struggle. We
had sent a message to other collaborators: "You will not get away with
hunting and killing Jews." More importantly, we had disrupted the
German spy ring in our area. This bought us time to establish bases
from which to operate.*

*As partisans our main objective was to make hit-and-run attacks
against German convoys who were carrying military supplies to the*

German armed forces. We blew up railroads and bridges. We disrupted German lines of communication. We never disguised our Jewish identity, and we chose to fight as an independent Jewish partisan fighting unit. I rose through the ranks to become the youngest lieutenant and platoon commander in our unit.

We also helped defeat the German army. On July 22, 1944, our units joined up with the Russian army in a village called Kainki, in the area of Lublin, Poland.

Family Camp

In the forests of Byelorussia, Lithuania, and Ukraine, another form of partisan group formed, the family camp. Unlike other partisan groups, family camps accepted older men, women, and children.

One of the best known was the Bielski Atriad, begun in 1941 by Tuvia Bielski and his brothers Zusya, Aharon, and Asael. They turned no one away, including older men, women, and children, whom other groups would not take in. The camp had nearly 1,300 fighters and many civilians. The group kept moving its location and successfully fought and eluded the Nazis and local antipartisan groups. In 1944, after the Russians liberated their territory, the Bielski Atriad became part of the Soviet army.

chapter five

Spiritual Resistance

In addition to physical resistance, a number of people engaged in spiritual resistance to the Nazis. Spiritual resistance was the unwillingness to accept Nazi definitions of time and human worth, among other things. This could be as simple as remembering that it was the Sabbath, or refusing to mistreat a fellow inmate in a camp. Educating oneself and celebrating one's culture were also spiritual resistance.

In the ghettos and some camps, cultural activities continued, usually in secret. Artists, musicians, actors, and singers kept creating and performing. Poets wrote of the suffering going on around them. Children in the Theresienstadt camp were encouraged to paint and write. Secret libraries and schools were set up. Children forbidden to attend real schools kept up their studies. They would hide books under their coats or make do without them. People in hiding would teach their children to read and write and to understand their religious heritage. In this way, Jews resisted the Nazi idea that they were worthless and sustained their lives and culture.

At other times, spiritual resistance was defined as holding firmly to the belief that, no matter how powerful the Nazis were, God was still in control and would hear His people. Countless people prayed silently. *Minyanim*, groups of at least ten men, gathered to pray in bunkers or anywhere else they could.

Rabbis set up underground *yeshivot*, schools where young men studied the holy books of the Torah, in hidden bunkers. Rabbis also tried to give guidance to people who asked agonizing questions about keeping Jewish law even in hopeless conditions. For example, could you save your own life—or your child's—at the expense of someone else's life? At least one rabbi refused to answer this question, knowing how tragic the outcome would be either way.

Whatever was available or could be smuggled in to keep religious observance was used. Margarine placed in potato peelings could be used as Sabbath candles. Many women made the blessing of the Sabbath candles on the electric lights of the concentration camp barracks. All of these acts were forbidden by the Germans. They testify to the Jewish belief that life is precious and holy, and must be preserved.

Non-Jews undertook spiritual resistance as well. Many Polish priests were imprisoned at Dachau, and some secretly celebrated Mass. Jehovah's Witnesses imprisoned at Neuengamme concentration camp continued to study and teach their beliefs. They smuggled in their official magazine, the *Watchtower*. One Jehovah's Witness was caught reading it and then refused to give up his religion. He was executed.

Religious Observance

Moshe Aftergut was only fifteen when he was sent from his town, Przemysl, to the Plaszów work camp. He recalls that the Jews there were somehow able to obtain a *shofar*—a ram's horn to blow on Rosh Hashanah, the Jewish New Year.

The Jews who came from Hungary still had civilian clothes and could smuggle in items. A great scholar, Mr. Mendel Brachfeld, brought a pair of tefillin *for prayer. People stood in line to put them on quickly and say their daily prayers. You can imagine what would have happened if they had been caught.*

Our barracks were divided by profession: tailors, shoemakers, upholsterers, all working for the Germans. I worked with the furriers, making coats for Germans going to the Russian front. I'll

תלמידי באבוב מוצלים מאש
ניו-יארק שנת תש״ח
RESCUED STUDENTS IN U.S. THROUGH EFFORTS OF BOBOWER RABBI

Orphaned teenaged boys and men pose for a photograph together. This group and others were brought to the United States after the war as a result of the work of Rabbi Halberstam, the Bobover Rebbe.

never forget Yom Kippur [the Jewish Day of Atonement], when the men and women recited the Kol Nidre prayer and said their prayers, all the while doing their work.

In the next barrack the upholsterers managed to take out three mattresses and stand them up, covering them with branches or twigs to make a sukka—*a booth for the religious festival of Succoth. So one would go inside and make a blessing while another would watch out for Goeth.*

Amon Goeth, who was portrayed in *Schindler's List*, was the camp commandant at the Plaszów concentration camp. He was known for killing Jews on a whim.

Religion Lost and Found

Moshe lost his parents and all of his brothers and sisters in the Holocaust. Like many other young survivors, religion became a difficult issue once he had been liberated from the camp. Moshe credits Rabbi Halberstam, known as the Bobover Rebbe, with his spiritual and physical survival after the war.

I was in Bari, Italy, with other orphaned teenagers. He brought us visas to come to America. We found in him a teacher, a father, a psychologist. He had to be very careful. Some of us were very emotional. Especially seeing little children playing in Italy, seeing mothers and fathers. It was a miracle that you were human, that you didn't break down. You had lost everything. Little by little, he brought us back to religion.

Many Jews who experienced the Holocaust became secular and anti-religious. Still others respected their religion but never returned to it.

A Final Gesture

Many of those who practiced spiritual resistance, like those who fought with physical weapons, did not survive the Holocaust. But a few of the 6 million Jews killed by the Nazis were able to confront their murderers with a last gesture of rebuke or humanity, even when all hope of life was lost.

One girl being led to her death in a group of Jews saw the typical cruelty of a German guard, who pushed people into the pit on top of each other. She turned and slapped him hard in the face. An old woman is remembered because she comforted a crying motherless child and even succeeded in making the child laugh before the Germans killed them both.

Others died with the words "*Shema Yisrael*"—"Hear, O Israel," the first words of the holiest prayer in Judaism—on their lips, giving strength to those who witnessed their death. Most confusing to the Germans were those Jews who used their last moments on earth to dance with joy, knowing that they would soon reach the next world, as long as they maintained their fervent belief in God.

chapter six

Living Testimony

In the ghettos, in the camps, in the forests and against all odds, some Jews and others were somehow able to resist the Nazis. It took many years for some Holocaust survivors to feel that it was all right for them to speak. They wanted to put the horror behind them. Some felt a deep sense of guilt because they survived but members of their family did not. Others wanted to speak out, but no one seemed ready to hear such horrors.

But now there is a sense of urgency. They are living testimony. They speak for themselves, but they also speak for the dead: their parents, grandparents, brothers, and sisters; children they knew and cared for or tried to help save; friends who sustained them; leaders whom they admired; strangers who offered them help when most betrayed them. The survivors remind us of countless heroic acts of resistance.

Resisters Today

The war ended in 1945, but the difficulties did not. Most of the people you've read about were orphaned during the war and had to grow up fast. Each had to struggle to rebuild his or her life after the war.

Abie Baron married Sari Stern, a survivor from Hungary, and they settled in the United States. They are active in their community and have two children and six grandchildren. Abie believes he survived for their sake and for the purpose of telling new generations what happened in the Holocaust. He sometimes speaks to school students, and they respond.

Frank Blaichman with his wife Cesia and their grandson.

Frank Blaichman served in the Polish government after the war. He briefly lived in Kielce, where in 1946, a year after the war, about forty-one Jews were killed in a pogrom. But Frank had left before that. "I married a Jewish girl who had also been a partisan, and we got out of there.

"For the past fifty years, I have tried to understand: What divine power enabled our group of partisans to become a successful fighting force? We were a terrorized group of young men and women who had become orphans overnight. Most of us were totally unprepared and untrained for combat." Frank and his wife live in the United States. They have two children and six grandchildren. He has become a successful businessman.

Leah Hammerstein married a fellow partisan, Yitzchak Silverstein. They moved to Israel before settling in the United States. She looks back on her own experiences. "As long as there is hate in the world, there will never be peace. We see it not only on the Jewish case. Look what's happened in former Yugoslavia, what happened in Biafra, what happened in India, what's happening in other places. You would think that people would learn something from what happened, but in my opinion, people didn't learn a thing. If you don't learn from your mistakes, you are bound to repeat them.

"Some people ask me, 'Do you think that the Holocaust is possible again?' My answer is yes, it's possible. You see, Nazism killed not only people: It killed moral principles. Before you can kill people, you first have to kill moral principles. Then it's possible."

Timeline

January 30, 1933	Adolf Hitler is appointed chancellor of Germany.
March 23, 1933	Dachau, the first concentration camp, is built to hold political opponents of Nazis.
April 1, 1933	Nazis proclaim a daylong boycott of Jewish-owned businesses.
July 14, 1933	Nazis outlaw all other political parties in Germany; a law is passed legalizing forced sterilization of Roma and Sinti (Gypsies), mentally and physically disabled Germans, African-Germans, and others.
January 26, 1934	Germany and Poland sign Non-Aggression Pact.
August 1, 1935	"No Jews" signs appear in Germany forbidding Jews from stores, restaurants, places of entertainment, etc.
September 15, 1935	German parliament passes the Nuremberg Laws.
March 13, 1938	Germany annexes Austria.
September 29, 1938	Munich Conference: Britain and France allow Hitler to annex part of Czechoslovakia in order to prevent war.
November 9, 1938	*Kristallnacht* (looting and vandalism of Jewish homes businesses and wholesale destruction of synagogues) occurs throughout Germany and Austria; 30,000 Jews are sent to Nazi concentration camps.
March 15, 1939	Germany invades all of Czechoslovakia.
August 23, 1939	Germany and Soviet Union sign Non-Aggression Pact.
September 1, 1939	Germany invades western Poland.
September 2, 1939	Great Britain and France declare war on Germany.
September 17, 1939	Soviet Union invades eastern Poland.

Spring 1940	Germany invades Denmark, Norway, Holland, Luxembourg, Belgium, and France.
March 24, 1941	Germany invades North Africa.
April 6, 1941	Germany invades Yugoslavia and Greece.
June 22, 1941	Germany invades western Soviet Union.
July 31, 1941	Reinhard Heydrich appointed to carry out the "Final Solution" (extermination of all European Jews).
Summer 1941	*Einsatzgruppen* (mobile killing squads) begin to massacre Jews in western Soviet Union.
December 7, 1941	Japan bombs Pearl Harbor; United States enters World War II.
January 20, 1942	Wannsee Conference: Nazi leaders meet to design "Final Solution."
Spring and Summer 1942	
	Many Polish ghettos emptied; residents deported to death camps.
February 2, 1943	German troops in Stalingrad, Soviet Union, surrender; the Allies begin to win the war.
June 11, 1943	Nazis decide that all ghettos in Poland and Soviet Union are to be emptied and residents deported to death camps.
March 19, 1944	Germany occupies Hungary.
June 6, 1944	D-Day: Normandy Invasion by the Allies.
May 8, 1945	Germany surrenders to the Allies; war ends in Europe.

Glossary

Aktion   A roundup of people (usually Jews) by the Nazis for deportation or transport to a camp.

Allied forces   British, French, Soviet, and U.S. armies united in Europe to fight Nazi Germany during World War II.

antisemitism   Hostility toward, hatred of, or discrimination against Jews.

Aryans   According to Nazi ideology, a person of Nordic or Germanic background, a member of Hitler's "master race."

bunker   A secure hiding place, usually below the ground.

collaborators   Non-Germans who willingly helped or supported the Nazis.

concentration camps   Places where political prisoners and prisoners of war are confined.

crematorium (plural: crematoria)   Oven in Nazi concentration camps and death camps used to burn the corpses of inmates.

death camps   Concentration camps where people considered unfit for work or racially undesirable are murdered.

deportation   The forced removal of people from their homes to labor camps, concentration camps, or other places of imprisonment.

dissidents   People who disagree with the ideas of the group that governs or controls a country or region.

emigration   The act of leaving one country to move to another.

gas chamber   A large locked room in which people were murdered on a mass scale by the use of the poison gas Zyklon B.

genocide   The deliberate destruction of one ethnic, political, religious, or cultural group.

Gestapo   The Nazi secret state police.

ghettos   Overcrowded, run-down, usually sealed sections of cities designated for Jews.

Holocaust   The mass slaughter of Jews and other minorities during World War II.

inflation   An economic term usually describing a dramatic rise in the prices of goods and services.

Kapo A prisoner in charge of other prisoners in a concentration camp.

Kristallnacht Meaning the "night of broken glass," November 9, 1938, was a government-sponsored attack on Jews, resulting in the destruction of Jewish-owned businesses and synagogues.

labor camps A camp where prisoners were forced into slave labor to help the German war effort.

Lagerälteste A guard chosen from among the prisoners at a camp.

Nazis (National Socialist Party) A political party in Germany that based their ideas on feelings of racial superiority.

Nuremberg Laws German laws passed on September 15, 1935, that legalized antisemitism and stripped Jewish Germans of many rights.

occupation The control of an area by a foreign military force.

partisans Groups of people who banded together to fight Nazi occupation and persecution.

pogrom A violent demonstration of antisemitism, including attacks on people and property.

political prisoners People put in jail for their beliefs and opinions.

propaganda The spreading of ideas, information, lies, or rumors for the purpose of strengthening a cause or harming others.

rations An allowance of food for one day.

sabotage Deliberately destroying equipment or property belonging to an enemy or interfering with the enemy's actions.

Selektion A process at concentration camps where those considered fit for work were separated from those marked for death.

Sonderkommando Concentration camp inmates forced to strip and dispose of the bodies of the victims in the crematoria and gas chambers at death camps.

underground Taking place without the knowledge or permission of the government or other authorities.

World War I The war in Europe that lasted from 1914 until 1918.

World War II The most devastating war in human history, lasting from 1939 until 1945 and involving countries all over the world.

Zeilappelle The often cruel roll calls of inmates in concentration camps.

For Further Reading

Altschuler, David A. *Hitler's War Against the Jews*. West Orange, NJ: Behrman House, 1978.

Drucker, Malka, and Michael Halperin. *Jacob's Rescue: A Holocaust Story*. New York: Bantam Doubleday Dell, 1993.

Eisenberg, Azriel. *The Lost Generation: Children in the Holocaust*. New York: Pilgrim Press, 1982.

Eliach, Yaffa. *Hasidic Tales of the Holocaust*. New York: Random House, 1988.

Frank, Anne. *Diary of a Young Girl: The Definitive Edition*. New York: Doubleday, 1995.

Holliday, Laurel. *Children in the Holocaust and World War II: Their Secret Diaries*. New York: Washington Square Press, 1994.

Jules, Jacqueline. *The Grey Striped Shirt: How Grandma and Grandpa Survived the Holocaust*. Los Angeles: Alef Design, 1994.

Klein, Gerda. *All but My Life*. New York: Hill & Wang, 1995.

Marks, Jane. *The Hidden Children: The Secret Survivors of the Holocaust*. New York: Ballantine Books, 1993.

Matas, Carol. *Daniel's Story*. New York: Simon and Schuster, 1996.

Rochman, Hazel, and Darlene Z. McCampbell, eds. *Bearing Witness: Stories of the Holocaust.* New York: Orchard Books Watts, 1995.

Roth-Hano, Renee. *Touch Wood.* New York: Puffin Books, 1989.

Wiesel, Elie. *Night.* New York: Bantam Books, 1982.

Wilkomirski, Benjamin. *Fragments.* New York: Schocken Books, 1996.

For Advanced Readers

Asscher-Pinkhof, Clara. *Star Children.* Detroit: Wayne State University Press, 1986.

Baumel, Judith Tydor. *Unfulfilled Promise: Rescue and Resettlement of Jewish Refugee Children in the United States, 1934–1945.* Juneau, Alaska: Denali Press 1990.

Dwork, Deborah. *Children with a Star.* New Haven, CT: Yale University Press, 1991.

Edelheit, Abraham J., and Herschel Edelheit. *History of the Holocaust: A Handbook and Dictionary.* Boulder, CO: Westview Press, 1994.

Gilbert, Martin. *The Holocaust: A History of the Jews of Europe During the Second World War.* New York: Henry Holt & Co., 1985.

I Never Saw Another Butterfly: Children's Drawings and Poems from Theresienstadt Concentration Camp. New York: McGraw-Hill, 1964.

Noakes, J., and G. Pridham. *Nazism: A History in Documents and Eyewitness Accounts, Vols. I and II.* New York: Pantheon Books, 1984.

Videos

Holocaust: Liberation of Auschwitz
The liberation of Auschwitz was filmed by the Soviets. Commentary describes the selection process, the medical experiments, daily life at Auschwitz, and impressions of the liberation. Note: Highly graphic. (Available from Zenger Videos, 10200 Jefferson Boulevard, Room 902, P. O. Box 802, Culver City, CA 90232, (800) 421-4246.)

More Than Broken Glass: Memories of Kristallnacht
Using archival footage and photographs and interviews with survivors, this video explores the persecution of Jews in Germany before and during the Holocaust. (Available from Ergo Media, Inc., P. O. Box 2037, Teaneck, NJ 07666; (800) 695-3746.)

Opening the Gates of Hell
American liberators share their memories of liberation. Interviews are combined with photos and footage showing camps liberated by Americans: Buchenwald, Dachau, Landsberg, Mauthausen, and Nordhausen. Note: Highly graphic. (Available from Ergo Media, Inc., P. O. Box 2037, Teaneck, NJ 07666; (800) 695-3746.)

Safe Haven
This video profiles America's only refugee camp for victims of Nazi terror. Nearly 1,000 refugees were brought to Oswego, NY, and incarcerated in a camp known as Fort Ontario for eighteen months. (Available from the Anti-Defamation League, 823 United Nations Plaza, New York, NY 10017; (212) 885-7700.)

Shoah
This film includes interviews with victims, perpetrators, and bystanders, and takes viewers to camps, towns, and railways that were part of the Holocaust. (Available in most video stores and many libraries.)

Web Sites

Anti-Defamation League—Braun Holocaust Institute
http://www.adl.org/Braun/braun.htm

Holocaust Education and Memorial Centre of Toronto
http://www.feduja.org

Museum of Tolerance
http://www.wiesenthal.com/mot/index.html

Simon Wiesenthal Center
http://www.wiesenthal.com/

United States Holocaust Memorial Museum
http://www.ushmm.org/index.html

Yad Vashem
http://www.yad-vashem.org.il

Index

About the Author

Charles (Bezalel) Anflick was born in Philadelphia, grew up in Fairfield, Connecticut, and now lives in Brooklyn, New York. He has been writing since the second grade. He studied in a Jerusalem yeshiva for several years. He has taught, edited schoolbooks, and written and performed in plays. He currently counsels people with mental illness at a social services agency and is studying for his master's degree in social work at Fordham University.

About the Series Editor

Yaffa Eliach is Professor of History and Literature in the Department of Judaic Studies at Brooklyn College. She founded and directed the Center for Holocaust Studies (now part of the Museum of Jewish Heritage—A Living Memorial to the Holocaust) and designed the Tower of Life exhibit at the U.S. Holocaust Memorial Museum. Professor Eliach is the author of *Hasidic Tales of the Holocaust; We Were Children Just Like You; There Once Was a World: A Nine Century Chronicle of the Shtetl of Eishyshok;* and *The Liberators: Eyewitness Accounts of the Liberation of Concentration Camps.*

Photo Credits

Cover photo Stanislaw Szmajzner, Yaffa Eliach Collection donated by Center for Holocaust Studies, Museum of Jewish Heritage, N.Y.; pp. 7, 26–27, 47 © courtesy of Yad Vashem Jerusalem; p. 8 © courtesy of the Leo Baeck Institute, New York; p. 11 © AP/Wide World; pp. 12-13, 32–33, 34, 45 © National Archives, courtesy of United States Holocaust Memorial Museum (USHMM) Photo Archives; pp. 14-15, 16, 41, 46 © courtesy of Archive Photo; p. 17 © George J. Wittenstein, courtesy of USHMM Photo Archives; p.18 Leah Hammerstein Silverstein, © courtesy of USHMM Photo Archives; pp. 18-19 © Main Commission for the Investigation of Nazi War Crimes, courtesy of USHMM Photo Archives; p. 20 © Jerzy Tomaszewski, courtesy of USHMM Photo Archives; p. 21 © courtesy of USHMM Photo Archives; pp. 22-23 © State Archives of the Russian Federation, courtesy of USHMM Photo Archives; p. 24 Stanislaw Szmajzner File, Yaffa Eliach Collection, donated by Center for Holocaust Studies, Museum of Jewish Heritage, N.Y.; p. 25, Eliezer Zilberis, © courtesy of USHMM Photo Archives; p. 28 © Benjamin Meed, courtesy of USHMM Photo Archives; pp. 36, 37, 38, 53 © courtesy of Abie Baron; p. 39 © Eliyahu Mallenbaum, courtesy of USHMM Photo Archives; p. 42, 53 © courtesy of Frank Blaichman; p. 50 © courtesy of Moshe Aftergut.

Series Design
Kim Sonsky

Layout
Laura Murawski